GREENHOUSE GARDENING
FOR BEGINNERS

The Basics of Greenhouse Gardening
for Growing Vegetables, Fruits and Herbs at Home
& Hydroponic for Beginners

GREEN THUMB COLLECTION
GARDENING IDEAS

TABLE OF CONTENTS

Introduction

A greenhouse is a structure with large transparent walls and a roof that is used to cultivate plants. The inside of a greenhouse that receives direct sunshine is substantially warmer than the outside temperature, shielding the plants from harsh circumstances.
The greenhouse is an excellent feature of any garden. It is great for seed planting, cultivating sensitive crops such as cucumbers and tomatoes, and overwintering delicate plants. Additionally, you may cultivate greenhouse or conservatory plants that benefit from the year-round protection provided by a greenhouse.

There are several factors to consider while locating and selecting a greenhouse. Continue reading for guidance on selecting, placing, and constructing a greenhouse, as well as maintaining it properly - including installing an automatic vent opener, guttering, cleaning, heating, and insulating it in the winter.
Modern smart greenhouses are equipped with heating, cooling, and lighting technology and are networked to a computer to optimize growing conditions for plants. However, let us examine the history of greenhouses.

History of greenhouse

Since Roman times, the notion of cultivating plants in environmentally controlled settings has existed. Tiberius (AD 14–37) consumed a cucumber-like vegetable every day, necessitating the development of artificial means akin to a greenhouse system for growing it year-round.

The earliest mention of artificially heated greenhouses dates all the way back to the 1450s in an agricultural journal created under Korea's Joseon kingdom. The paper's part on winter vegetable cultivation includes directions for creating a greenhouse using ondol, a traditional Korean heating system installed under the floor. Insulated walls and clear windows provide just enough light for plant development while also protecting against the elements.

The idea of greenhouses originated in the 17th century in the Netherlands and England. In 1681, the very first stove-heated greenhouse was erected in the United Kingdom at Chelsea Physic Garden for the purpose of growing medicinal plants.

Innovations with greenhouse design flourished in Europe throughout the 17th century, as technology advanced and building skills improved. Their grandeur and potential are shown by the ornate and gigantic greenhouses at the Palace of Versailles, completed in 1789.

Greenhouses made their way to America in the 1700s. In 1737, Andrew Faneuil, a successful Boston businessman, constructed the country's first greenhouse. George Washington constructed a greenhouse at his Mt. Vernon estate to serve pineapple to his visitors.

Charles Lucien Bonaparte, a French botanist, is credited with building the first effective greenhouse at Leiden, Holland, in the early 1800s. He used it to produce tropical, therapeutic plants.

Initially, greenhouses were exclusively available to the wealthy, but their research potential extended to colleges, where they started to sprout up.

Other significant 19th century greenhouses include the Munich Glaspalast, the New York Crystal Palace, which was initially created as an exhibition space, and the Royal Greenhouses of Lueken, which were erected for Belgian King Leopold II.

In 1880, Samuel Cocking, a European trader who traded herbs, created Japan's first greenhouse.

Recent history

In more recent years, the geodesic dome has gained popularity as a structure for many sorts of greenhouses. The Eden Project in

Cornwall, England, and the Cimarron in the Missouri Botanical Garden in St. Louis, Missouri, are two prominent examples.

The 1960s saw the introduction of bigger sheets of polyethylene film, the evolution of greenhouses, and the widespread use of hoop houses by farmers. As production prices decreased, small farms and garden shops started to see an increase in greenhouses. The durability of polyethylene films rose dramatically in the 1970s with the development and use of more powerful UV-inhibitors; they raised the film's usable life from one or two years to three, and ultimately four or more years.

The Future

In the future, technology will expand to improve the way food and other plants are grown in greenhouses. Artificial intelligence (AI) and machine learning are the inevitable future of climate-controlled greenhouse farming in order to feed a hungry world.

Chapter 1 Is Adding a Greenhouse to Your Garden a Good Thought?

Greenhouses may be both attractive and functional constructions for gardeners. If you have ever wondered if it would be worthwhile to build or purchase one for your garden, we have some views to help you weigh the benefits and drawbacks.

1.1. Purpose of greenhouse

Greenhouses act as a barrier between nature and the plants you are cultivating, extending, and maybe improving growth seasons. They protect against extreme cold or heat, as well as bugs. While we used the phrase in jest, the term "greenhouse effect" in reference to our planet is a more complicated and serious matter for our global ecology, the impact of a greenhouse on plants may be very beneficial for the home grower. The purpose of a particular sort of greenhouse is to produce a space that retains heat. The structure obstructs the passage of thermal energy out, and sunlight passing through the translucent "walls" of a greenhouse heats the earth within, radiating warmth and warming the air. Alternatively, if excessive heat is an issue, a greenhouse may assist you in creating or regulating a more temperate climate for plants by including a cooling device.

1.2. Types of Greenhouses

The sort of greenhouse you need is determined by your location and the type of plants you want to cultivate. Greenhouses are classified in several ways.

Temperature - The following sorts of buildings are available in response to the ambient temperature requirements:

Hot House (Temperature: above 60°F) Tropical plants are maintained in hot greenhouses. They need extra heat to stay warm.
Warm Houses - (Temperature: 55°F) Supports the survival of a wider variety of plants throughout the chilly winter months.
Cool Houses – (Temperature: 45-50°F) This sort of greenhouse will sustain temperatures above freezing, allowing for the survival of plants that would perish in severe cold.
Cold House– (Temperature: Falls below freezing) Provide shelter for plants; however, temperatures may still fall below freezing in this sort of greenhouse due to the absence of an extra heat source. Cold houses are used to lengthen the growing season in the spring by enabling crops to be started earlier and extending the growing season in the autumn by helping crops grow longer.

There are several other issues within each of these broad categories. There are very basic greenhouses and extremely complicated greenhouses. The more technology is used, the more precise the regulation of growth circumstances, from temperature to water and moisture levels. Greenhouses may also be created without walls to reduce direct sunlight (a shaded greenhouse) or merely a screen to keep insects away.
Materials — For the home gardener, the options are almost limitless. Price and aesthetic factors and your aim are likely to influence part of your decision-making on this. Each has its own set of pros and downsides.

Options for support or framework include plastic, aluminum, wood (which rots quickly), and iron. Certain types have curved eaves, while others have straight eaves.

Glass is the costliest but lasts the longest and is also the most attractive, plastic (cheap but effective), fiberglass (may discolor), double-layered polyethylene (must be replaced every 2 to 3 years), acrylic (very expensive), and PVC.

Design - Additionally, greenhouses may be assessed on the basis of their design style. It is the enjoyable part. Several typical styles of greenhouse "design" include the Dome, A-Frame, Lean-To (which may even include a garage or home wall as one of the sides), Gothic (arched), and Quonset.

Environmental Quality Options - Your budget will have an effect on what you can achieve in this area. Automatic controls are perfect for greenhouses but are costly basic room heater, pressured heat, radiant heat, hot or steam water systems, as well as soil warming pipes under plants are all viable possibilities for heating equipment. Automatic plant watering systems are desirable for bigger greenhouses. Ventilation planning is also critical for the health of your plants.

Chapter 2 Choosing a greenhouse

There are several factors to consider when selecting a greenhouse, notably size and material. Aluminum is more affordable and durable than wood, which is more costly and retains heat effectively but requires care. The majority of people regret not purchasing a larger greenhouse; therefore, get one as large as your finances, and available space allows.

A greenhouse is a must-have for every serious gardener; it is great for seed sowing, cuttings, growing sensitive plants and crops, and overwintering fragile plants. There are several alternatives available when it comes to greenhouses, and costs range from a few hundred to many thousands of dollars. The greenhouse you ultimately pick will be determined by two primary aspects: the available space and your budget.

Prior to doing anything else, choose a location - this will limit the amount of greenhouse that may be installed.
Moreover, you will need to determine if you can lay the foundations and construct the greenhouse yourself or whether you will need to have it built. We explain how to pick a greenhouse and the elements to consider. Once you have decided on a greenhouse, you will need some equipment - learn more about the necessary greenhouse kit and the finest greenhouse accessories. Alternatively, if you are seeking

outdoor storage space rather than growing space, we have compiled a list of the finest garden sheds, along with detailed guidance on what to consider before purchasing.
However, you now have the thrilling possibility of selecting a greenhouse.

2.1. What to look for when purchasing a greenhouse?

There are several alternatives available when it comes to greenhouses, and costs range from a few hundred to many thousands of pounds.

Dimensions

Greenhouses are available in a variety of lengths and widths, in increments of two feet. Choose one that is at least 6ft wide and 8ft wide that allows for staging (or shelves) on both sides. The eaves should be at least 5ft (1.5m) tall to allow for enough light. The majority of gardeners wish they had a larger greenhouse, so pick the largest you can afford and fit in your space.

Design

The classic greenhouse, the octagonal greenhouse, and the lean-to greenhouse are the three primary greenhouse forms. Additionally, newer designs such as domes are accessible. Lean-to's make use of an existing wall, such as one on the south side of a home or garage.

The bricks retain the sun's heat, particularly at night, which is great for growth. A dome or octagonal form is advantageous if you have an awkward area.

Metal or Timber greenhouse?

Aluminum is a low-cost material that requires little maintenance and may be powder-coated in a variety of colors. Timber, often cedar, is more appealing but also more costly and requires more maintenance. It is more effective in sustaining a consistent temperature. Wood models may be completely glazed or half-walled with lumber or brickwork. This effectively retains heat but precludes the growth of plants at ground level.

Choosing the ideal location

Finding the ideal location for your greenhouse is critical. You will need a flat, sunny location free of frost pockets and chilly winds. It should ideally be located on an east-west axis to maximize light, particularly during the winter. Discover the six critical factors to consider for the site selection of a greenhouse.4

2.2 Placing and Constructing a greenhouse

Constructing your own greenhouse may save you hundreds of pounds — and the larger the building, the more money you will save. Along with construction expenditures, you may save money by leveling the land, creating foundations, and laying routes inside. If you are interested in giving it a try, read our advice on greenhouse construction.

The location of a new greenhouse or polytunnel might be the difference between success and failure in terms of growth; thus, it is critical to get it properly.

Of course, there could be only one location for your greenhouse, but if you do have a choice, it is worth locating it optimally. You will require a location that receives the lightest and sunlight and is free of frost pockets and chilly gusts.

While it may seem counterintuitive to give up a prime location or an already productive area of your garden, when you consider the greater benefits – being able to thrive crops all year, prolonging the growing season, helping to raise seedlings, and overwintering delicate plants – the sacrifice is well worth it.

You will require a location that receives the lightest and sunlight and is free of frost pockets and chilly gusts. Avoid constructing your greenhouse on a sloped surface. Although theoretically conceivable, it would complicate matters since the staging inside must be horizontal. Definitely avoid placing it near the foot of a hill since this is often a frost trap where cold air persists - not ideal for winter growth.

East to west orientation of your greenhouse

If you wish to produce crops all year, aligning the structure's ridge east-west is ideal since this maximizes winter light. Additionally, it will assist it in heating up more rapidly after chilly nights. If you want to produce primarily summer crops, aligning the ridge north-south is ideal since it ensures that each side receives an equal amount of light and helps prevent overheating on the warmest days.

Ascertain that enough space exists around your greenhouse.

Ascertain that there is at least 1m of space around your construction. Not only does this facilitate installation, but it also comes in handy when panes or coverings need to be replaced, as well as while cleaning or just strolling through. Leaving this area also means that fences and other structures will be able to throw shadows and obstruct airflow.

Provide a healthy soil environment in your greenhouse.

If you want to plan directly in the beds of your construction, find a location with adequate soil if possible since you will be putting a lot of strain on it. Poor soil may be addressed by digging organic stuff into it and raised beds may also be an option. Avoid stony or rocky land since these might complicate the building process.

2.3 Greenhouse glazing

Horticultural glass admits the maximum amount of light, is durable, and can readily be replaced if damaged. Although toughened glass is more costly, it is a better choice in high-traffic areas or if you have children. It still shatters, but more safely. Polycarbonate is less expensive, stronger, and more insulating than acrylic but allows less light through and may burst out of its frame in severe winds.

Ascertain that your greenhouse receives enough light.

By purchasing a greenhouse from a provider and erecting it yourself, you may save hundreds of dollars on construction expenses – and the larger the structure, the more money you will save. Additionally, you might save money on land leveling, foundation construction, and route laying inside the greenhouse. None of this is beyond the capabilities of an experienced do-it-yourselfer, particularly given that all greenhouses include comprehensive instructions.

Although the building abilities needed are elementary, proper preparation is critical. To begin, prepare the site by leveling it and laying the foundations. Using fences or screens is worthwhile if you are building on an exposed location or just wish to disguise the project.

Once the greenhouse comes, thoroughly inspect the kit to ensure that all of the components are there. Read the instructions thoroughly to ensure that you understand how the construction fits together. Assemble a greenhouse with the assistance of two or three individuals.

By purchasing a greenhouse from a provider and erecting it yourself, you may save hundreds of dollars on construction expenses – and the larger the structure, the more money you will save.

You Will Require:

- Supplier's greenhouse kit
- Hammer
- Foundations of brick, concrete, or slabs
- Spirit level
- Spanners that can be adjusted
- Screwdriver

Duration:

A weekend

First step

Whether you are using an existing base or constructing your own out of concrete, paving slabs, or brick, the foundation must be leveled.

With a spirit level, check that it is flat and that the opposite sides are the same length (if they are not, the glass panes will not fit). When constructing a foundation, verify the frame's actual measurements before beginning although these dimensions are sometimes quoted as 8x10ft or 6x8ft, they are a rough estimate, and frames are typically larger.

Second step

It is a good idea to separate the clips and bolts before you begin to avoid losing them. Arrange the frame's components, construct each portion, then join them together. Then transport the components to your foundation and secure them in place using screws. Secure roof sections, roof bars, and corner strengthening bars, but be careful not to overtighten. At this point, you are only keeping everything together until the glass is added, at which time more modifications may be necessary.

Third step

After assembling the door, attach the door runners after the remainder of the frame is done. Then move the door onto the higher track, followed by the bottom track. Adjust the top track's height until the door operates properly. This is an excellent opportunity to add automatic window openers and louver vents if you already have them. These contribute to maintaining an equal temperature within the greenhouse, minimizing summer heat waves that might sear fragile plants.

Fourth step

Using foam rubber strips or glazing tape, line the glazing frames. These will act as a cover between the greenhouse body and the glass and act as a cushion between the panes. A glass may be used to ensure that your corners are even, and the spirit level can be used to ensure that everything is level. This will guarantee that the glass is supported firmly and tightly. First, glaze the roof. You should be able to move freely inside and outside the structure while you are gazing. Install the wall panes after the roof is in place.

Fifth step

Tighten it up as you construct — you must constantly check the bars with a spirit level. It is critical to maintaining square uprights and horizontals; otherwise, the glass will not fit properly. You may find that you need to make small tweaks along the way. After installing all of the glass, return to the area and tighten all of the bolts. Take care not to over-tighten since bolts might break, and the glass may even fracture. After securing everything above ground, it is time to tighten the foundation fittings.

Chapter 3 Ventilation & heating in the greenhouse

Ventilation is critical during the hot months. Automatic vent openers ensure that your greenhouse's ventilation is continually maintained, whether you are at home or not, and they are fast and simple to install if your greenhouse does not already have one.

Maintaining a cool greenhouse throughout the summer is critical since excessive temperatures may induce heat stress, resulting in plant and crop damage. Dampening and darkening the space using shades, screens, and shading paint may assist, and it is critical to promote proper air circulation by opening doors and vents.

By installing an automated vent opener, you can ensure that your greenhouse ventilation is regularly controlled throughout the hot summer months, whether you are at home or not. It includes a wax that swells upon heating, thereby allowing the vent to open. When the temperature drops, the wax contracts, so closing the vent.

UPVC greenhouses often feature lightweight roof vents that may need a stronger vent opener to keep them closed or from blowing away - verify before you purchase. Automatic vent openers, which are available at garden stores and online, are simple to install — here's how.

Requirement:

- A Greenhouse
- Screwdriver
- Kit for automatic ventilation
- Screws

Time required:

- 2 hr

Directions

- Set the opener in the middle of a window vent and make a note of the hole locations on the window and greenhouse frames. The center may already contain pre-drilled holes when you have a steel greenhouse.

Or else, use a pencil to mark the location on the metal and drill the holes.

- Attach the automatic window adjuster to the window frame and test that the window opens and closes properly.
- Customize the proportion the window opens if required by spinning the vent opener's main tube.
- On a bright day, observe and wait to ensure that the vent is adequately opening.

3.1. Heating the greenhouse

Shielding your greenhouse with bubble wrap can help your plants survive the winter while still allowing light to enter. A maximum/minimum thermometer and a greenhouse heater might be beneficial while overwintering plants. Read our suggestions on how to keep your greenhouse warm throughout the winter. A greenhouse may be essential for protecting sensitive plants from the elements in the winter. Additionally, you can utilize your greenhouse in the winter to grow herbs, winter salads, and citrus trees, as well as sow early seeds.

1. Purchase polythene bubble wrap

By insulating your greenhouse with bubble wrap, you can keep frost away while still allowing light to enter. Fit bubble-wrap panels into the greenhouse windows. Bubble insulation wrap is available in large rolls – typically 75cm wide – in stores and online.

2. Construct 'dual glazing.'

Apply overlapping layers of bubble wrap to a greenhouse's wooden frame. Pin overlapping layers of bubble wrap to a greenhouse's wooden frame. Trim the sheets to length, but instead of reducing the breadth, insert the excess polythene behind as an additional layer. This holds the polythene away from the window, trapping an air layer between the glass and sheet, reducing heat loss — similar to double glazing.

3. Eliminate draughts

Connect bubble-rap sheets with transparent, waterproof tape. For gap-free joints between the insulating sheets, use transparent weatherproofing tape. Carefully wrap the sheets over vents to eliminate draughts. Seal holes in glass and, if required, repair seals around doors.

4. Make a curtain

To partition a greenhouse, create a bubble-wrap curtain. Partition your greenhouse into smaller zones by using bubble insulation as an inside curtain. Fix securely around the roof and sides, all the way down to the floor, and secure it with something heavy. Once installed, you will notice that tiny spaces often keep warm without the use of heaters.

5. Add heat just as necessary.

Add a heater for a greenhouse. Turn heaters on only when they are required and off when not. An electric fan heater with a changeable thermostat is a suitable alternative if you have access to power. If not, paraffin heaters are advantageous. Each evening, replenish the gasoline tank.

6. Utilize a maximum-minimum thermometer.

Utilize a max & min thermometer to determine if heaters are operating properly. You may install a digital temperature sensor in the greenhouse and connect it to your home's display monitor. Check the temperature periodically, particularly during cold times, to ensure it stays at your preferred level.

7. Essential kit

Greenhouse staging elevates plants off the ground, preventing contact with colder air, and provides a handy working height. Slats improve air circulation, which helps prevent fungal growth. Propagators aid in seed sowing success; a heated propagator or mat accelerates germination and roots.

3.2 Dampening

It can become exceedingly heated on summer's scorching, sunny days. Although greenhouse crops such as tomatoes, aubergines, cucumbers, and melons benefit from heat, excessive heat may shock them and induce tissue damage. Above 27°C, damage may begin - you may see leaf burn, wilting, or withered young foliage. Warm temperatures may also impair pollination and destroy growing fruits.

In the summer, dampening down the greenhouse and putting water over the greenhouse floor is critical. It maintains sufficient moisture during the day to protect your plants from heat stress. In the peak of summer, there are 3 things you can do to keep your greenhouse nice:

provide shelter from direct sunshine, offer proper airflow, and dampen down. Additionally, it is critical to maintaining plants well-watered.
To guarantee proper ventilation of the greenhouse, open all vents and doors early in the morning; this will assist in keeping the greenhouse cooler. Provide shade with shutters, netting, or shade paint to keep plants cool.

Dampening down means merely putting water over the greenhouse's bottom. Do this first thing in the morning — as the water evaporates, it will provide enough moisture throughout the day to keep your plants cool. Additionally, it aids in the reduction of red spider mite infestations, which prefer a dry atmosphere.
Here's how to properly dampen your greenhouse.

Requirement: Watering container

Directions

- Whenever the weather prediction calls for hot, dry weather, sprinkle water on the greenhouse floor early in the morning. It permits the water to gently evaporate throughout the day, replenishing the air with much-needed moisture. If necessary, repeat throughout the day.

Chapter 4 Installation of Guttering

Installing guttering and a water catchment system not only conserves water but also enables you to simply fill your watering container for your thirsty crops throughout the summer. Plastic guttering kits are readily accessible at any home improvement shop. Manufacturers of greenhouses often provide custom-made gutter kits for their own products, and many greenhouses come equipped with guttering. If you are refurbishing an existing greenhouse and know the manufacturer's name, contact them first to see if they can offer a kit before visiting a DIY shop.

Guttering is reasonably priced and may be trimmed to length with a saw. You will also discover a range of connections and brackets, so bring your greenhouse's dimensions with you when you go to get your guttering to assure you have the correct components. Attach the brackets into the greenhouse's frame to secure the gutter, which has an end stop on one end and a downpipe flowing water into the butt.

You can still attach guttering to a metal-framed greenhouse. Rather than screwing straight into the wood, most will come with pre-drilled holes for attaching guttering, or you may drill your own. If the structure already has guttering, all that is required is the addition of a downpipe to route the water into a water butte.

Installing gutters and water butts to collect rainwater is an excellent approach to conserve this limited natural resource.

Requirement:

- Downpipe
- Guttering lengths
- Brackets joined
- Brackets for gutters
- Saw
- Screwdriver
- Screws
- Chicken netting

Time required:

- 2 hr

Directions

- Measure and cut gutter lengths to fit neatly along each side of your greenhouse.
- Mount brackets at regular spacing throughout the frame, each slightly lower toward the downpipe to create a flow of water.
- Fit the guttering into the hooks with care. Join lengths of guttering together using connecting brackets with waterproof rubber seals for a secure fit.
- Fill the gutter with water to ensure that it flows freely toward the drain line and that there is no leakage.
- Insert the downpipe into the butt and secure the top with a piece of chicken wire to prevent leaves from falling in.

4.1. Gutter cleaning in greenhouses

Avoid placing your greenhouse directly under trees. They will throw a shadow, encouraging the growth of green algae and further limiting light, while fallen branches and leaves may cause harm and clog gutters. Honeydew from insects on tree leaves may cause glass or plastic to become sticky and filthy. Additionally, tree roots may wreak havoc on the foundations, making planting straight into the beds within difficult.

Maintaining a clean greenhouse allows the greatest amount of light to penetrate (particularly crucial in the winter) and reduces the likelihood of pests and illnesses hiding. Spring and fall are the best times to clean before and after the primary growing season.

Winter is an excellent time to clean, tidy, and rearrange your greenhouse since it will be relatively empty, and there will be fewer garden tasks competing for your time. Cleansing the greenhouse increases light levels, unclogs gutters, and eliminates pests and illnesses. Cleaning things up now will ensure that you have an orderly work environment in preparation for the next growing season.

Choose a moderate day to securely put any overwintering plants outdoors for a bit. It is recommended to refill water butts and increase the light sources for overwintering plants to prevent them from becoming tall and leggy.

Additional techniques for organizing and cleaning your greenhouse are included below.

Requirements:

- Sponge with a long handle
- Bucket
- Broom
- Glass cleaner
- Sponge for cleaning
- Disinfectant

Time required:

- 1 day

Directions

- If you are overwintering sensitive plants, choose a moderate period to totally clear your greenhouse. If required, cover plants or bring them indoors. Clean the framework and stage, followed by sweeping the floor.
- When everything is outside, make a commitment to yourself that you will not return anything that is not absolutely necessary.
- Your greenhouse windows will need cleaning on both the interior and exterior. Utilize a bucket, sponge, and long-handled sponge to thoroughly wipe over each window with a glass cleaning solution to soak up and scrape away grime. To reach the glass in high ridges, use a solid platform or a stepladder
- Examine your gutters for accumulated leaves and debris that may filter into water butts. Brush away trash before it enters the downpipes. Replace the guttering that has to be repaired.

- Dump the water butts and wash out any filth that has gathered in the bottom, then replace them. If you do not already have a water butt, now is an excellent time to install one - it will provide a convenient supply of water on hot days.
- Wipe surfaces clean with a scouring sponge and disinfect flowerpots and seed trays before completely washing. Restore order to the greenhouse by returning everything outdoors to its appropriate location.

Chapter 5 Essential Greenhouse Accessories

Greenhouses are a fantastic method for gardeners to build their own microclimate and grow crops such as spicy peppers, delectable tomatoes, and aromatic herbs. They enable you to cultivate an array of intriguing culinary and decorative plants and lengthen the growing season, which is wonderful news for garden lovers. If you are considering investing in a greenhouse, we have put together a useful guide that contains all the information you will need to make an informed decision.

After constructing your greenhouse and stocking up on greenhouse spares such as tunnel sheeting and more greenhouse clamps, you can begin kitting up the inside.

There are several beneficial greenhouse accessories that will assist you in creating the optimal planting environment and enhancing your growing experience. If you are seeking gardening gift ideas, the products below also make excellent greenhouse presents. Consider the following selected selection of essential greenhouse shelves, tools, and equipment.

1. Greenhouse staging or shelves

The metal staging is ideal if you seek more growing areas and require greenhouse shelves or greenhouse tables. Made of rust- and rot-resistant aluminum, it is durable and low-maintenance, with a slatted surface that promotes air circulation and allows water to drain easily.

2. Thermometer with maximum & minimum settings

With this handy thermometer, you can keep track of the highest and lowest temperatures in your greenhouse, as well as the relative humidity in the area. Knowing the exact settings of your greenhouse will enable you to create an atmosphere that is ideal for your plants. This greenhouse thermometer comes with an integrated stand or can be placed on the wall and is powered by a single AAA battery.

3. Heater

Heaters will keep your greenhouse warm over the winter, allowing you to continue growing and nurturing your plants. Additionally, it will enable you to regulate the temperature throughout the year and avoid abrupt changes in the weather outside from harming the conditions within your greenhouse. According to the company, this eco-friendly version consumes the same amount of energy as a regular light bulb, which is 25% less than conventional tube heaters.

4. Container for watering

A watering can is a critical greenhouse accessory since it is used to water individual plants whenever they need it.

5. Shading

Appropriate shading in a greenhouse may make a world of impact for plants that need some shade. These roller blinds come in groups of two or four and adhere to the glass with easy suction cups, allowing you to simply move them to any area that requires shade.

6. Tidy tray

A gardening tray functions similarly to a little portable potting bench, storing compost while you work and being simple to clean and put away when finished. Garden trays are lightweight and durable, with a low lip in the front for easy access to your work area.

7. Seed trays

Seed trays are very helpful greenhouse accessories since they are ideal for propagating and nurturing new plants.

8. Compost scoop

A dependable scoop is essential for all planting on and transplanting tasks. Rust-proof stainless steel scoops are weatherproofed ash grip that is ergonomically engineered for comfort and durability.

9. Watering system using drip feed

By providing your plants with just the water they need, an automated drip watering system may save you time and energy while also helping to preserve water. The solar-powered system can irrigate up to 20 pots and does not need a tap connection; all that is required is a tank filled with water that is then brought to your plants through the drippers.

10. Plant trays

Trays are great for collecting water, dropping leaves, and compost from your pots when placed on top of greenhouse tables or shelves. The staging trays are made of strong, molded plastic and may be filled with gravel or clay particles as well. There are two sizes available, 'jumbo' or 'giant,' depending on the number of pots you require.

11. Capillary matting

Capillary matting is a valuable greenhouse attachment that keeps water in touch with your plants at all times. It is a dense, fuzzy substance that is extremely absorbent and, when put in the base of trays and moistened, will assist in keeping the roots of your plants wet. Mattings are sold in single packs of 2 meters by 60cm sheets.

12. Propagator

If you want to jumpstart your greenhouse plants, a heated propagator is a way to go. This propagator from Suttons maintains a steady, automatically regulated temperature and has three segregated areas to help avoid the spread of damping-off and other air-borne illnesses. The lids are vented, allowing you to regulate each environment independently.

Chapter 6 Pros and Cons

After immersing yourself in an incredible amount of knowledge regarding the enormous array of possible greenhouse designs, let us explore some of the reasons you would want to do this - or not.

6.1. Pros of Having a Greenhouse

- Fresh cut flowers all year round
- Fresh greens, vegetables, and fruit
- A warm place to go in the middle of a cold, grey winter

- There will be no more encounters with squirrels or insects
- Transplant availability and success

ability to grow things that you could not before (tropical fruit, exotic flowers)

- Do more of what you like for a longer period of time. Enhance the aesthetics and visual attractiveness of a landscape

6.2. Cons of a Greenhouse

- Can be costly to heat
- Construction may be costly
- Could raise electricity and water expenses
- Constant maintenance, monitoring, and care are required
- May detract from a garden's visual appeal

Your greenhouse garden may be built extravagantly or inexpensively, out of plastic or glass, to resemble a beautiful glass home or to serve a useful purpose. Finally, the choice to purchase a greenhouse will be determined by whether you feel the greenhouse will enrich or subtract from your life.

Chapter 7 Purchasing a Used Greenhouse

Used greenhouses may be advertised in a newspaper's classified advertising section. Purchasing a secondhand greenhouse is an excellent method to save money while getting the ability to plant year-round. Purchasing used greenhouses is an excellent method to save money. When evaluating a greenhouse, four criteria should be considered: size, condition, materials, and pricing. Weighing these aspects carefully will assist you in selecting the ideal greenhouse for your growing requirements and budget.

Size:

When selecting the size of a used greenhouse you need, it is typically a good idea to pick one large enough to accommodate all of your plants and tall enough for you to walk about freely. Taller greenhouses are also advantageous since they are easier to heat in the winter and ventilate in the summer. Numerous gardeners have difficulties later on, as they continue to add plants and finally run out of room. They then add modifications that are often more costly than first acquiring a bigger product. As a result, selecting a little bigger model than you need is typically a wise choice.

Condition:

It is critical to obtain a secondhand greenhouse in excellent shape. Avoid purchasing anything with corrosion or fractures in the frame or coating. These are a definite indicator of wear and tear and will eventually result in a shorter lifetime, which means spending more money on replacement components in the future. Before making a purchase, you should do an in-depth inspection of the used greenhouse from the inside out.

Materials:

The materials utilized in a used greenhouse might vary significantly, and there is no one optimum choice. Galvanized steel and aluminum are the most durable frame materials. These are suitable due to their durability and resistance to the weather. Plastic frames are often a bad option because of their structural fragility and susceptibility to heat loss.

It is generally better to avoid glass when choosing a covering since it is brittle and sometimes has problems keeping heat. Typically, plastics such as polycarbonate and polyethylene film are ideal because of their shatter resistance and low maintenance requirements. Polycarbonate is available in a single, double, or triple thickness, while polyethylene is available in a single or double thickness. Generally, it is recommended to use the thickest covering available since this will minimize heat loss.

Cost:

The last element that will affect your choice is the cost. Generally, you may anticipate spending between 25% and 70% less than the typical retail price. Generally, it is prudent to shop about and inspect many greenhouses before coming to a decision. Comparing and contrasting your alternatives by doing an online or classified ad search for a used greenhouse may be an efficient technique to compare and contrast your possibilities.

Chapter 8 Structures & Designs of Greenhouses

Currently, greenhouses cover approximately 1.4 million acres of land worldwide. We will examine these structures, identifying the many types and the characteristics that distinguish them.

As you consider purchasing one, keep in mind that various kinds of greenhouses are better suited to certain plants, functions, and conditions. As a result, the sort of greenhouse you pick will be mostly determined by your unique requirements. Additionally, some will perform better in some conditions than others.

One of the most common ways to categorize a greenhouse is by its structural style or form. Each construction offers many advantages and disadvantages that should be considered before making a purchase. Additionally, you may classify greenhouses according to their outside covering and frame material.

8.1. Categorization of Greenhouses According to Their Structural Style or Shape

There are several greenhouse kinds, and one method to classify them is by their structural form. This category includes the following:

1. Ridge & Furrow Greenhouse

An excellent example of greenhouse structural types is the ridge and furrow structure, which mimics an A-frame structure. The plan will involve neatly aligning the A-frame components. Each row is connected at the eave, which is the drainage location of all surplus snow and rain. This specific style is used on big farms with several greenhouses that need protection from rain and snow. The connecting of many greenhouses increases the growth area as well as the space available for increased sunshine penetration. Additionally, this reduces the cost and energy required to care for plants as they move from greenhouse to greenhouse.

Pro

- Reduces automation and energy consumption.
- Provides enough space for plants inside the building.
- An attractive appearance.
- Extends the life of the building by draining rain and snow off the roof.

Cons

- Requires a large plot of land.
- Expensive to establish.

Example of Ridge & Furrow Greenhouse

Outdoor or Indoor Mini Walk-In Green House

You will note the greenhouse's distinctive A-frame construction, which may be configured as a ridge and farrow. All you have to do is connect the greenhouse's sides and open the ends to make one enormous area. The frame structure is constructed entirely of high-quality aluminum that is sturdy and corrosion resistant. Additionally, the A-frame roof construction offers enough heat dispersion to support the growth of all plants.

2. Lean-To Greenhouse

This type applies when a greenhouse is attached to the side of a building. You may use the wall as one of the greenhouse's sides or sandwich it between two structures. This leaves three or two sides and the roof to cover with greenhouse sheet material to create a complete enclosure. The majority of lean-to greenhouses do not surpass 12ft in height and can only accommodate one or two rows of plants at a time. However, if necessary, you may stretch it against a longer wall as long as it receives enough sunshine.

Pros

- A more compact construction results in lower material costs.
- Convenient access to utilities such as power and water from the main building.
- Reduced roof support needs.
- Requires just a tiny amount of room to set up.

Cons

- Is not exposed to adequate light for healthy plant development.
- Offers a small amount of plant space.
- Height restriction imposed by the supporting wall.
- Temperature regulation is difficult due to the wall sides.

3. Even Span Greenhouse

The two different sloping tops of these greenhouses make them clearly distinguishable. You may easily utilize this design to construct a tiny greenhouse in your garden based on your specifications. While assembling it, you may consider either connecting one end to the house or allowing it to stand alone in the garden. Additionally, you may build it as large as possible to accommodate additional rows and racks that hold a variety of plants. Each space is encased in clear glass or another transparent material, allowing plants to get enough sunlight. Yet, heating such a large area might be more expensive. You may need the installation of a heating system to prevent temperatures from dropping during the winter days and nights.

Pros

- Spacious enough to accommodate a large number of plants.
- A design that is adaptable to your size.
- A-frame roof prevents rain and snow accumulation.
- An excellent shape that ensures temperature homogeneity.

Cons

- Requires a self-contained heating system.
- Expensive to establish.

4. Greenhouses with Gothic Arches

Consider any gothic edifice you have ever seen, and you will have a good idea of what a Gothic arch greenhouse looks like. It has a distinctive pointed roof, which helps avoid the requirement for trusses in the building. Due to the fact that this construction may be as little or as large as desired, it is perfect for both hobby and commercial applications.

All you need to do is keep track of your space and costs to choose the size you want. Additionally, consider the advantages and disadvantages of Gothic arch greenhouses before making a decision.

Pros

- Visually appealing.

Versatile in terms of size, since it may be large or little.

- It eliminates the need for trusses.
- It facilitates the drainage of snow and rain.

Cons

- It prevents adequate air circulation to the corners.
- It consumes more resources than other forms of greenhouses.

5. Greenhouse with an Uneven Span

When it comes to the unequal span greenhouse, you will notice a distinguishing aspect. The term derives from the fact that one of the roofs on this construction is longer than the other. The fundamental objective for the construction of this building is to maximize sunlight reception when the structure is located in hilly terrain.

Typically, the roof's lengthier side faces south and must be clear. Given that most greenhouses are now located in flat locations, this greenhouse style is becoming less prevalent.

Pros

- It aids in the transmission of sunlight to the plants.
- Sturdy and durable construction.
- Prevents wind from blowing in.

Cons

- Not recommended for flat regions.

8.2. Categorization of Greenhouses by Frame Material

Each greenhouse needs a solid frame construction to provide you with the best assistance. Without the proper materials, the frame will deteriorate over time and may simply collapse. As a result of this classification, you will have the opportunity to learn about the best materials to use on various kinds of greenhouses.

1. Greenhouses with Wooden Frames

7

The majority of cold-weather greenhouses have timber frame designs that aid in retaining heat inside. The majority of them are tiny backyard installations used to keep plants till spring. Wood is widely accessible in a variety of locations and is quite straightforward to deal with, even if you do not hire an expert to construct the greenhouse.

Pros

• Simple to construct and repair.

• Thermal efficiency enables the greenhouse to maintain a comfortable temperature throughout the chilly winter months.

• Timber framing is more eco-friendly.

• Wood is inherently beautiful, particularly when the visible grain is present.

Cons

• If not maintained correctly, it is prone to pest attack.

• Wood is costly when it is not supplied locally.

2. Polycarbonate Greenhouses

Tough plastic may be used to construct a high-quality greenhouse, particularly one that is kept inside and out of direct sunlight. When considering various kinds of inexpensive greenhouses, you may want to consider ones constructed with plastic frames. Due to the low cost of the material, you will not have to go over budget while putting one up.

Pros

• They are simple to clean.

• Sturdy frame constructed of high-quality plastic.

• Plastic greenhouses are cost-effective.

• They are not as susceptible to damage as wood greenhouses.

Cons

• Plastic frames are not well-suited to supporting massive constructions.

8.3. Categorization of Greenhouses based on Material Coverage

Different kinds of greenhouses are covered with a variety of materials. This dictates the sort of greenhouse that is employed in certain places. Additionally, depending on your area, the following resources are available.

1. Metal Pipe Frame Greenhouses

Numerous pipe-framed greenhouse buildings are constructed from heavy-duty metals like as aluminum and steel. These metals are durable, which means you may use the greenhouse for an extended period of time.

If you choose a metal pipe frame construction, be cautious to research the metal utilized since some are prone to corrosion. Additionally, if the greenhouse is to be used commercially, it is prudent to choose robust metal since this decreases the expense of repairing worn pipes.

Pros

- Provides a weather-resistant framework.
- Made of a strong metal substance.
- Metal frame constructions are resistant to heat, even at elevated temperatures.

Cons

- Heavy-duty metal is an investment.

Examples of Metal-Pipe-Frame Greenhouses

Waterproof Quitrent Greenhouse:

This style of greenhouse is constructed using pipes made of a heavy steel alloy material. Not only is it robust, but it also protects the structure from corrosion. Additionally, it has a high-quality PVC covering that protects from harmful UV rays while providing an ideal atmosphere for growing plants within. Moreover, it takes little time to set up and transfer your plants. Additionally, the little greenhouse may be used both inside and outdoors.

Hopewell Walk-in Greenhouse:

With six shelves and three levels, this greenhouse is another excellent choice for indoor or outdoor usage. The structure is constructed of alloy steel, which is strong and will not bow under the weight of the plants. Nonetheless, the structure is portable and offers adequate shelf space for potted plants.

2. Greenhouses Made of Glass

Glass is another high-quality material that is often used to cover various kinds of greenhouses. It enables a greater intensity of light, which is good for healthy plants. Additionally, it provides adequate air filtration, the most effective way to manage the humid climate.

Pros

- Visually appealing.
- Allows for adequate air filtering.
- Increases light penetration.

Cons

- Glass is costly to employ, much more so on a large greenhouse.

Example of Glass Greenhouses

Indoors, you can quickly set up this tiny glass greenhouse and grow succulents. It maintains the ideal humidity level for plant growth. Also, glass is the finest material for light penetration, making it perfect for plants that need a lot of light.

3. Polyester Plastic or PVC Material for Greenhouses

PVC plastic is a very common material for greenhouse covers. It is translucent, which is necessary to ensure that sunlight reaches the plants. Additionally, it saves you money on greenhouse costs and heating

Pros

- It is compact and simple to assemble.
- Easily accessible.
- It is inexpensive.
- Allows for maximum light penetration.

Cons

- Susceptible to harm after a period of time.

Example of PVC greenhouse

Completely Self-Contained Walk-In Greenhouse:

This walk-in greenhouse is constructed of high-quality PVC material that allows maximum light penetration. It may be used both inside and outdoors. The frame structure is constructed of heavy-duty steel, ensuring that it is solid and durable. Inside, you will find eight shelves for storing plants, and you will not need any equipment to assemble them.

Worth Garden Walk-in Greenhouse:

The building is sufficiently long and broad to walk inside and tend to the plants. It is wrapped in high-quality PVC to shield plants from damaging UV radiation while allowing for enough light penetration. Additionally, the exterior frame is heavy-duty metal, which maintains its strength even when all three levels are brimming with potted plants.

Chapter 9 Hydroponic - A New Way to Grow Indoor Plants

Hydroponic is a type of agriculture in which plants are cultivated in nutrient solutions rather than earth. The greenhouse and its climate management system are identical whether plants are produced hydroponically or traditionally. The greenhouse must be production-ready, with appropriate air and heat circulation and the capacity to control both and clean glass for optimum light. The distinction between hydroponic and traditional production lies in the support system for plant growth and the technique used to feed water and nutrients.

In recent years, the cost of energy, labor, and agricultural inputs has soared. Gardeners are increasingly adding hydroponic veggies to their harvests to optimize return on investment. Sustainably grown vegetables and fruits are a better investment and use of resources and time.

Growing prospects for greenhouse producers to improve earnings and sales utilizing existing year-round facilities have risen. Hydroponics is simpler and more dependable than field gardening. Low agriculture input and labor costs, good quality. Converting greenhouses to food crops may be simple and inexpensive. Hydroponically grown crops in existing greenhouses have a bright future, given the vast market potential and cheap investment costs.

9.1. Why Diversify?

A typical greenhouse grower may produce bedding plants, foliage plants, blooming potted plants, and cut flowers. The most common greenhouse regimen is costly and frequently difficult to afford. They now confront growing competition and escalating labor, energy, and agricultural input costs. Local tomatoes, lettuce, peppers, and cucumbers are in great demand; thus, producers are rapidly expanding their crops to incorporate hydroponic veggies. Sustainable and local food is a big subject. Many producers have learned that year-round greenhouse vegetables and fruits are profitable.

School districts & restaurant franchises are switching to locally sourced meals. States are boosting the amount of fresh fruit in school

meals to help children and teachers live healthier lives. Consumers are becoming more concerned about the origins of their food, which will increase demand. Transporting food by air, sea, or truck has become impractical due to rising transportation costs and food safety issues. With all of this in mind, it should be evident that buying local is the way to go.

9.2. Benefits of Hydroponics

Growing prospects for greenhouse producers to improve earnings and sales utilizing existing year-round infrastructure have risen. But the reluctance of producers to include vegetables and fruit is puzzling. Using a pre-existing greenhouse is simple.

Hydroponics is simpler and more dependable than field gardening. Low labor and agriculture input costs, good quality. For a one-crop-per-year harvest, hydroponic and greenhouse yields frequently exceed field yields. Hydroponic and greenhouse harvests have surpassed field yields in several circumstances. One California grower produces 3.2 million blooms per acre!

Soilless hydroponic cultivation may raise greenhouse sales six or more times per square foot. It is now extremely simple and inexpensive to convert greenhouses to culinary production. Growers may convert current low- to medium-tech greenhouses to hydroponics without purchasing a new greenhouse. Many growers can do it themselves with sufficient knowledge and perseverance.

A rising number of universities and vocational institutions provide agricultural programs to prepare students for careers as enthusiastic farmers. Banks and other major players in the local food trend will stand with this new crop of producers. Many new and established farmers have secured low-interest loans from institutions that understand the economics of these enterprises. From corporate CSA programs to locally farmed food in lunchrooms, meetings, and conferences, producers rapidly acquire advocates beyond the agriculture sector.

Hydroponically growing in existing greenhouses has a promising future. The low cost of investment and practically limitless market potential have prompted clever producers to cultivate more edibles as a fraction of overall growing space.

Why wait till Spring to Start out Growing Hydroponically!

There's never been a sweeter or more exciting moment to get started with hydroponics. More than ever, producers seek answers to issues that have troubled farmers for centuries, and hydroponics may be the finest option yet.

If you want to lower your greenhouse running costs, prolong your growing season, and increase your earnings, contact us to learn more about hydroponics. It could be the finest choice you make all year.

9.3 Ways Hydroponic Greenhouse Can Help You Save Money

If the first "agrarian revolution" started when humans began cultivating crops in soil, the second might occur when we began removing them from the soil entirely. Of course, we are referring to hydroponics - the ground-breaking, soil-free way of producing fruits and vegetables that have sparked a fresh surge of enthusiasm in the agriculture world.

One important reason for the surge in interest in hydroponics is that the majority of current systems are intended to improve profitability while simultaneously lowering long-term expenditures. Hydroponic technology has a lot to offer tomorrow's gardeners, whether via resource conservation or the elimination of historically time-consuming manual work. Here are just a few of the primary ways hydroponics is assisting farmers in lowering long-term running expenses and why it may be time to upgrade your produce operation to a hydroponic system.

1. Enhance Water Efficiency

Generally, a grower dealing with plants in typical earth soil may anticipate losing a substantial amount of the water they sprinkle over the plants to drainage. Not only may this result in leaching and degradation of local water sources, but it also signifies an inevitable loss of operational income.

Because hydroponics removes the need for soil or ground planting and instead uses water as the primary growth medium, they make it substantially simpler for farmers to decrease water runoff and increase water conservation season after season. Each drop of water in your hydroponic system is utilized to the utmost degree possible without sacrificing gravity or other hungry plants.

2. Decreased Diseases 7 Invasive Pests

The soil remains a primary vector for illnesses, pests, and other dangerous pathogens to access your plants in practically every conventional grow operation. Whether as a result of runoff from another impacted field or just the natural process of soil health, in-ground cultivation nearly always exposes plants to diseases and pests– while hydroponics may assist in accomplishing the reverse. A hydroponic setup is a closed system, which means that there should be no simple access or exit routes for molds, pests, illnesses, or other pathogens to reach your plants.

As you and your farmers follow industry-standard cleaning and sanitation measures between plantings, the crops should stay substantially less susceptible to pests than soil-grown crops. This translates into huge cost savings in terms of pest control and a greatly decreased chance of loss due to illness or contamination.

3. Maximize Revenue-Generating Area

One of the most frequent issues we hear from producers is their inability to strike a balance amid "too much useless ground space" and "insufficient area for plants to flourish." Add to it the typical unproductive area seen in many conventional grow operations and achieving that sweet spot in regard to profits-per-square-foot may be challenging.

That is why hydroponic systems, with their modular spacing and highly effective use of the horizontal ground area, can significantly increase square-foot productive capacity within a high tunnel or greenhouse structure. By eliminating unused space in favor of clean, concentrated grow areas, producers can produce larger and better harvests while using the same percentage of ground space.

4. Increase the number of profitable plants

Once you decide to sow your plants in the ground, you often have to limit yourself to the most likely crops to prosper in your location. Not all soils are suitable for producing grapes, for example, and in very cold or storm-prone places, even simple crops may be more difficult to cultivate. On the other hand, hydroponics does not depend on external circumstances to function successfully. That implies that with the correct hydroponic system, you can produce even more lucrative crops than ever before, maximizing profit per square foot and minimizing energy loss during harvest.

5. No Weeding Is Required

Diseases and pests are not the only intruders trying to prey on your crops as they develop. Weeds may invade your crop beds quicker than you can pick them out when they are planted in soil. This may gobble up time, work, and attention that you would not have otherwise. Since hydroponic systems are soilless and confined, weeds have little opportunity of establishing a foothold in your crops. As a result, you will have more time to focus on making your produce as attractive and abundant as possible rather than worrying about invasive weeds and other natural invaders.

6. Increase Harvest Size and Reliability

While the capacity to produce crops in the offseason and lower the probability of crops being lost to illnesses or pests may save you

money on its own, increasing the amount and quality of your harvest will also help you increase your profits-per-square-foot.
Hydroponics enables farmers to achieve exactly that, often increasing harvest dependability and quality via enhanced nutrition and water delivery. As each plant has straight root access to whatever it needs to develop and flourish, your greenhouse has a far higher chance of producing larger and better yields than it could in the soil.

7. Four-Season Agriculture

For far too long, producers have been constrained by shifting seasons and unpredictable weather when determining when and where to plant their crops. In northern climes or locations prone to storms, this has typically meant restricting the growing season to spring and early summer or limiting the kind of crops that can be effectively cultivated in the fall and winter seasons. Due to the fact that hydroponic systems allow for consistent management of ventilation, temperature, humidity, fertilizer levels, and other elements on a daily basis, hydroponic gardeners do not need to restrict their winter or fall crops to those that thrive in cold weather. Allow yourself to produce tomatoes in January - they may even come out juicier than ever before, owing to your hydro system.

8. Automate & Reduce Labor Costs

The cost of labor required to carry a crop bed from seed or a shoot to harvest is a significant strain on any grower's budget. This job might range from cleaning and pest control to merely monitoring and modifying environmental controls to maintain ideal conditions. Automating the hydroponic system may significantly minimize the effort required to obtain the same – or even better – outcomes.

Everything from the grow room temperature to the humidity and light levels to the fertilizer levels, and quality can be automated in a hydroponic system, ensuring optimal delivery even while you are miles away from your greenhouse. That is because automated systems can continuously monitor and adjust for changes in conditions in your grow area, saving you the time and effort required to monitor and react to issues in your grow space.

Chapter 10 Identifying and Resolving Typical Greenhouse Issues

A healthy crop cycle under glass requires the capacity to detect and resolve numerous difficulties throughout the greenhouse. In a horticulture operation, many things may go catastrophically wrong. With so many factors to consider, a grower must prepare for a slew of regular issues as well as unforeseen occurrences and shocks. As a grower, you must also be able to think of problems before they happen and be able to quickly troubleshoot them so that they do not become a bigger problem. If you are troubleshooting or just being preventative, here are some frequent concerns you could face in a greenhouse, as well as solutions.

Common problem No. 1: Greenhouse temperature swings

The summer of 2020 brought record-breaking temperatures to the entire state of California, including both the south and north areas. Death Valley in Southern California hit 135 degrees, the highest temperature recorded in over 95 years. In some areas of the state, radiant temperatures (which are described as net radiant heat gain or energy loss and vary from ambient temperature) reached 125 degrees in September, exacerbated by wildfires and smoke.

Using such intense environmental temperatures, one feasible solution that does not need more air conditioning capacity is to moderate

overly hot environmental conditions, including radiant and ambient temperatures, with shade cloth or a greenhouse whitewash.
A whitewash is achieved by applying one or more applications of non-permanent, washable white, paint to the greenhouse glass.

Whitewash may be used instead of a cleaning solution in operations that employ automated glass washing equipment. Whitewash may also be applied by helicopter in certain larger-scale projects.
While the purpose of whitewashing is to lower radiant temperatures, it also has an effect on the quantity of photosynthetically active radiation (PAR) light that reaches the field. If light levels fall below goal, try washing the paint off and reapply fewer coats or a more diluted paint mix. Finally, while deciding how much light and radiant heat to take out of the greenhouse, producers must compare the hazards of heat exposure against the loss of light.

A heating system is required in colder areas. An inefficient heating system may be costly at best and deadly at worst. If farmers are experiencing chilly areas in the greenhouse or lower overall temperatures and checks for leaks and holes where cold air may be invading have been performed, the heating system could be at fault. The early spring is the optimum time to completely evaluate and repair any heating systems. Prior to wintertime usage, all heating equipment and thermostats should be repaired and inspected—it is better to avoid a problem in the autumn than to deal with one in the thick of winter.

Common problem No. 2: Air filtration

Greenhouses are often forced air/positive pressure settings rather than sealed settings (such as hybridized facilities with glass ceilings). This implies they should have air filtration and sterilizing characteristics on both the inlet and exhaust air. For diseases and pests protection, the input air is filtered and sanitized. A good ventilation system also enables a grower to regulate vapor pressure deficit (VPD) to some extent.

Clogged air filters, which reduce airflow, are typical of these systems. Greenhouse operators may use wind speed sensors to identify whether airflow is being curtailed. Fortunately, bigger automated ventilation equipment often includes sensors that notify producers when to change filters. However, air filters should be tested on a regular basis and replaced as needed. The placement of the operation will decide how often filters must be replaced — do not depend entirely on manufacturer suggestions for when to replace the filters since each case is unique.

Common problem No. 3: Constant mold and pest problems

Aside from the general operation of the watering or fertigation system, sanitation is a top responsibility. Pythium and other disease vectors may be spread through polluted irrigation equipment and/or contaminated water. If farmers continue to have Pythium issues throughout several crop cycles, try decontaminating the whole watering system, including pipes and the water reservoir (if a water tank is used). Again, this would be done after each crop in a perfect world.

Water tanks and irrigation lines may be disinfected using the same water and hydrogen peroxide mixture. Schedule a water supply disinfection after an irrigation cycle, so when the tank is mainly empty, then fill the tank with the 20percent concentrated solution.
If the irrigation system has been sanitized, but the problems continue, it may be time to thoroughly clean the greenhouse.

Common problem No. 4 Watering and fertigation systems.
After harvesting and in between the crop cycles, it is ideal to diagnose, replace or repair, any damaged, worn out, or malfunctioning fertigation or watering equipment.
To establish if a fertigation system is working correctly, monitor the flow rate. Growers should ideally have a standard to compare against that was originally assessed when the equipment was deployed. Reduced flow might indicate a blocked dripper, filter, or dosage meters. Wilting plants are a clear indication of a possible watering issue. Meanwhile, in the case of automatic irrigation systems, a computer should alert producers to a problem before it becomes visible in the plants.
"Planning proactively about future greenhouse concerns will be the distinction between a humming business and a squandered investment."
Growers may clean the irrigation network with water and hydrogen peroxide combinations if the flow rate is lowered. When flushing systems, use a mixture of up to five parts waters to one part hydrogen peroxide. This may be done between harvests as a prophylactic measure.

Producers or output team members should also manually inspect each dripper to ensure there are no obstructions that the peroxide cleaning agent did not remove.

Common problem No. 5: Crops drying out

If crops seem to be continuously dehydrated, evaluate any connected electrical controls concerned for timing, watering, and cycles for mechanical faults or blockages to avoid over or under watering or failing to water on time.

Thinking ahead of time about possible greenhouse difficulties and preparing how to prevent or handle such problems will be the distinction between a humming business and a squandered investment. With this in mind, create SOPs that instruct team members on how to do things correctly and what to do if things go wrong.

Common problem 6 No. increase in EC/nutrient levels

Consider inspecting the fertigation lines if there are substantial increases in nutrient solution electrical conductivity (EC) (which farmers would see in runoff testing), yet levels are normal at the solution supply. Fertilizer salts may have formed. In addition, properly examine nutrient application equipment like injectors for EC and flow rate to avoid under or over-fertilization problems from spreading and generating nutrient application difficulties.

Chapter 11 DIY Greenhouses

A couple of easy to make yourself greenhouses to get you the experience of what you might be missing out on.

11.1. Cedar Branch Garden Hoop House

This basic cold frame, or 'cloche,' acts as a mini greenhouse, protecting seedlings from frigid spring weather, and is withdrawn as soon as the climate warms. It may be adjusted at either end for optimal ventilation. It is durable enough to survive a strong wind or heavy rain yet light enough to be lifted and transported to another vegetable patch where fresh seedlings are placed. And most of all, it took 45 minutes to construct and required no resources. This is how it is done:

1. From a fir tree, cut six little curled branches.

If your location possesses cedar trees, they are great for this endeavor due to cedar's intrinsic resistance to decay. For this project, we utilized cedar, but you could also use short 'bendy' branches from most conifers. Curved branches should be clipped to around 6' - 7' in length. (If a bigger cloche is needed, use longer branches.)

2. Trim and sharpen the branches' broad ends.

Remove any branch spurs with nippers and sharpen the bottom end of each branch with a hatchet so it can be jabbed into the soil effortlessly.

3. Insert the ends into the dirt and bury them at least 12 inches.

Three hoops are used in this design. Plant the branch endpoints about 3' apart and 3' across from one another in the soil. If this is too difficult, your soil could be too dense. If your soil is suitably prepared for planting, you should have little issue pushing the edges into the bed.

4. Form a hoop out of the opposing branches and bind them together.

When assembling the branches, you may twist them around one another to create the curved shape. Now, bind both ends to the rings using numerous wraps of thread. We chose sisal for the string since it was readily available. A woven nylon string would be preferable due to its durability, but that is your option.

You may observe at this time that your hoops do not line properly at the top. That is acceptable; the following step will rectify the situation. At this level, there is no use in attempting to make it appear flawless.

5. Lashing a straight stick to the middle of each hoop along the top.

It is easy to construct your own custom-made cloche by using straight branches, such as an old broom handle, or even a 1" x 2" piece of timber (we made ours out of cedar). Simply put it along the top and fasten it to the hoops, making sure to align the ridge with the approximate center of each hoop. This ties the whole structure together and gives it a consistent appearance.

6. Form the cover by attaching the translucent plastic sheets.

Cut a sheet of transparent poly that is broad enough to wrap the hoops and long enough to reach about 18" beyond the cloche's ends. Spread the sheet over the frame and secure it with a few staples to the hoops at each end. Additionally, attach a few staples into the ridge. At this point, you may roll the excess plastic at either end to create the appropriate opening size. You are now completed!

Gently roll up the ends of the cloche to provide ample air for the plants. Roll down the ends for additional warmth when the weather becomes colder, or the evenings get frigid. Simply remember to reopen them when the sun comes out. Otherwise, you risk the cage scorching.

Once your seedlings no more need protection, simply remove the cloche. Simply not a string to the base of each rim at ground level, extend it over to the other side, and tie it off at the base. This should be repeated for each hoop. It is to prevent the hoops' bottom (in-ground) ends from springing outward when they are lifted from the earth. Once the hoops are secured at ground level, just raise the whole cloche up and transport it to the next bed. Loosen the plastic and detach the top ridge from the rims at the end of the season; the hoops may then be stored flat against each other in the shed without taking up much room.

Even though little cloche is designed to provide brief protection for seedlings, you may be amazed at how long it lasts. It will last for many years if you use a strong thread to tie it together, such as nylon twine. We still use the original "temporary" cloche we constructed over 30 years ago in our garden!

11.2. Cold Frame Greenhouse from An Old Window

How to create an interesting DIY cold frame- You can get different prototypes from suppliers and unique cold frames that include recycled windows as the lid. Additionally, you might use transparent plastic for the lid. The concept is that the glass or plastic will trap the warmth of the winter sun, enabling plants to flourish within. While we are not discussing tomatoes here, there are various other veggies and greens that you may plant. According to what I have read about cold frame designs, the rear should be around three to six inches taller than the front to maximize solar energy collection.

The following are the instructions for my do-it-yourself cold frame.

You may alter the dimensions to fit the size of the lid you are using. Keep in mind that the window should not include lead paint since this can flake off over time and end up in the soil.

Cold frame project plan

Tools

- circular saw or Jigsaw
- Hand saw miter
- Sandpaper or orbital sander
- Dozuki saw (Japan)
- impact driver or Drill press
- Pencil and straight edge
- Tape measure
- Protective eye and earwear
- Clamping devices (optional)
- Gloves for work

Materials

This project was designed to fit an existing window that measures 32 1/4'' long by 30'' broad

- two hinges
- 1 1/2-inch-by-6-inch-by-8-foot (4 cedar planks)
- 2 screws 3/4-inch
- (5 front and back parts)1 1/2 by 6 by 32 1/4inch
- (2 pieces with angled sides) measuring 1 1/2 by 5 1/2 by 30 inch
- 1 1/2 by 6 by 30 in. (4 side pieces),
- (2) 1 1/2 by 6 by 11-inch corner bracing (cut from the scrap)

- (2) 1 1/2 by 6 by 16 1/2-inch corner bracing (cut from the scrap)

1: Construct the frame

Arrange the 32 1/4-inch front and back sections so that they completely cover the 30-inch side pieces. Nail in place to form the frame's bottom. This process should be repeated to make the second layer. There is a rear part but no front part on the third layer due to the slanted slope you want to produce after the window is mounted. This requires an angle cut on the side sections. Additionally, they must be longer to meet the slope. Leave approximately 10 inches on end to secure the workpiece to your bench using screws or clamps when you do the cut. Fasten the side piece temporarily to the rear piece and set it on top of the box. Draw a line diagonally across the boards from the border of the upper corner towards the front of the box using a straight edge. Undo the interim screws and clamp or screw the additional 10-inch length to the worktable. Cut it out carefully across the grain with a circular saw or jigsaw. A single cut creates both bent side pieces. Trim the excess ten inches from the length of one piece.

2: Sand the side cuts

Smooth the jagged surfaces of the angled side parts using a sandpaper or an orbital sander.

3. Join the angled side parts

Insert the two angled side parts into the third back piece's edges and secure them in place from the rear. Due to the angle of the finished project, there is no front piece for the third level of this assembly. Add an additional screw on each side toward the front to lock the side pieces in place since they will not be connected to the corner bracing.

4: Install the corner braces

Cut two pieces 2 16 1/2 inches and two pieces 2 11 inches from one of the remaining cedar planks. The lengthy parts serve as back corner bracing. Trim the ends of these on an angle to match the mild slope of the angled side pieces' tops, or you may cut them shorter and place them below the angle. The window should shut completely without creating a gap below. Screw these four bracing to the exterior frame from the inside to hold it in place.

5: Trim the front of the plastic

If any wood from the two angled pieces overlaps the front, carefully cut it away using a dozuki handsaw or an orbital sander.

6: Glue the hinges in place

Because the pre-existing metal piece along the rear of the previous window would have blocked the screws for the hinges, two leftover pieces of wood were chopped and utilized to construct a new "back" to which the hinges could be fastened. This also shifted the window forward somewhat to compensate for the cm added by the diagonal. After screwing these pieces into place, join the two hinges to the window frame and the box frame.

Once you begin using your cold frame, it is essential to understand that temperatures might rise a bit too high inside, which is why it is necessary to give vent to the cold frame occasionally, even in the winter. I prop mine up with an old piece of wood, but you can also get automated vent openers that will detect the temperature and open appropriately.

Chapter 12 Greenhouse Seed Starting

Although many seeds may be placed directly in the garden in the autumn or spring and thrive on natural weather swings, others are far more sensitive and need consistent temperatures and a contained situation to germinate. Gardeners can offer a stable environment for seeds to sprout and seedlings to flourish by beginning seeds in a greenhouse. Continue reading to find out how to plant seeds in a greenhouse.

12.1. When Should You Plant Greenhouse Seeds?

Greenhouses enable you to manage the humidity and temperature needed for seed multiplication and the growth of young seedlings. Because of the regulated atmosphere, seeds may be started in greenhouses at any time. If you are growing plants to transfer into gardens outside in the spring, start the seeds in greenhouses six to eight weeks before the latest estimated frost date for your region. Most seeds grow best in temperatures ranging from 70-80°F (21-27°C), with nighttime temperatures not falling below 50-55°F (10-13°C.). Your greenhouse's temperature must be regularly monitored.

Greenhouses are normally warm in the day when the sun shines but may get much colder at night. Heat mats, especially designed for seeds, may assist in maintaining consistently warm soil conditions for seeds. Greenhouses with ventilation or opening windows help exhaust greenhouses that have become excessively hot.

Seed Starting in Greenhouses

Seeds are often started in greenhouses in flat open seed trays or single plug trays. Seeds are prepared according to their unique requirements, such as being soaked overnight, scarified, or layered, and then planted in containers in the greenhouse. Seeds are often sown in well-spaced rows in open flat trays to ease thinning, watering, fertilizing, and treating seedling illnesses like damping off. The seedlings are then transferred into individual pots or cells after they have produced their first set of genuine leaves.

In single-cell trays, just one or two seeds are placed per cell. Several experts believe that planting in plug trays is preferable to planting in open trays as the plug cells contain and maintain more moisture and heat for the growing seed. Seedlings can also remain in plug trays for extended periods without their roots getting entwined with those of their neighboring plants. Seedlings in plugs may be easily removed and replanted directly into the yard or container setups.

You do not need to spend a lot on specific seed starting mixes when beginning seedlings in a greenhouse. You may make your own multi-purpose potting mix by combining equal parts perlite, peat moss, and organic material (such as compost). However, it is critical that any potting material you use be sterilized between uses to remove microorganisms that might cause damping off, a seedling illness. Furthermore, if greenhouse temperatures are too chilly, light is not strong enough, or seedlings are overwatered, they may produce lanky, weak stems.

12.2. February Plants to Start Indoors

Kick off the gardening season right with a variety of plant seeds to sow in February. Seed envelopes provide information on planting schedules, sowing depth, and harvest dates, which might be useful for the home gardener who wishes to save money on seedlings or cultivate his own plants. The Old Farmer's Almanac recommends beginning seeds 4 to 6 weeks before the outdoors planting season. Plant the seeds earlier in the season to ensure a more developed plant for transplanting.

Vegetable Planting

Capsicum and Tomatoes need extensive growth seasons. Seeds should be started indoors in February and grown for 6 to 10 weeks. According to the University of Minnesota Extension, after the seedlings reach approximately 8 inches in height, harden them off for a week or two before transplanting them into the garden. Plant these warm-weather veggies when soil temperatures reach 60° F for the greatest results. To prevent transplant stress, use biodegradable containers since peppers detest having their roots disturbed.

Annuals such as chard, lettuce, and eggplant are among the crops to grow in the spring. According to the Missouri Botanical Garden, February is a wonderful time to start these plants inside and members of the Brassica oleracea family, which includes Brussels sprouts, cauliflower, cabbage, and broccoli. Squash should be started at the same time as the tomato and pepper plants.

Some plants, such as carrots, beets, and radishes, do not transplant well. If frost strikes, use hotbeds, cold frames, floating row covers, or other protective coverings to preserve these plants while sowing outside. Plant seeds in pots that may be transferred to more protective settings if required. Experienced gardeners collect detailed notes in order to create a customized vegetable growing season chart.

Fruit Planting

Watermelon, honeydew, and cantaloupe should be started inside due to the extended growing season needed by melons. While tomatoes and Cucurbita species such as pumpkins, squash, gourds, and cucumbers are often referred to as vegetables, they are really fruits. Cucumber seeds should be planted during the final week of February. Also, Pumpkins need a lengthy growth season and should be planted in February.

Strawberry seeds need about 6 weeks of cold storage before planting in February. When the seedlings have three leaves, they must be hardened off before being transplanted to their permanent growth location

Herbs & Flowers Planting

In February, start annual herbs such as dill, basil, and parsley. Parsley and basil are sensitive to chilly temperatures and cannot withstand temperatures below freezing. However, in general, the seedlings do well in pots on the porch or patio. Once the fear of frost has gone, you may also transplant the herbs straight into the garden.

Herbaceous perennials that thrive when started indoors including oregano, mints such as peppermint and spearmint sage, and thyme

Seedlings grow nicely in porch or patio planters well as directly in the garden. On the other hand, these perennials may need protection under severe winter circumstances.

Seed packages are far less expensive than flower flats at the greenhouse; in February, plant annual hybrid flowers such as New Guinea impatiens. During February, start herbaceous perennials such as pansies, heliotrope, and violas inside. Before planting immediately into flower beds, seedlings should be gradually exposed to outside temperatures for a week or two. When to transplant seedlings outside is determined by your growing zone or microclimate.

12.3 Grow Vegetables Year-Round in a Greenhouse

Yes, veggies can be grown in a greenhouse all year. Set up a separate tropical greenhouse or rotate among seasonal veggies. If you have a greenhouse, your year-round veggie garden layout will be less constrained by the seasonal change and weather. Because you can manage the humidity and temperature inside a greenhouse, you can sustain near-summer-like settings and enjoy a tropical garden all year. Regardless of technique, preparing and caring for vegetables and fruits inside a greenhouse necessitates a few alterations to your watering, fertilizing, and planting regimen, particularly if you will be producing food in containers.

Getting the Most Out of Your Greenhouse

It is critical to understand that simple greenhouses have certain restrictions. For example, the poor winter sunshine and early sunsets that pass through the greenhouse windows indicate to plants that the growing season has come to an end, and cold temperatures may still creep into the greenhouse and harm delicate foliage and flowers. You may not be able to grow hot-weather fruits and vegetables all year

unless you invest in supplementary heating and lighting to establish a tropical greenhouse.
Another critical element to consider is the scarcity of natural pollinators. Insects that naturally transport pollen from blossom to bloom will vanish in the winter, and they may have a tough time getting inside your greenhouse if you never open it. Learn about the pollination needs of the vegetables and fruits you intend to cultivate.

It may be as easy as putting up an oscillating fan to imitate wind, or it may be necessary to spread pollen by hand using cotton buds.
Finally, when you design your year-round vegetable garden, consider how to make the most of your greenhouse area. Set up a trellis system for vines and plant vegetables in pots that may rest on robust shelf units inside the greenhouse. You may also be thinking of hanging upside-down pots in the middle of your greenhouse. Take into account that using containers requires more regular watering and fertilization since the soil dries up quickly and nutrients seep out with each soaking.

12.4 Your Year-Round Garden Planning

Unless you want to install a heating system in your greenhouse to preserve summer-like temperatures throughout the winter, it is best to stick to seasonal planting dates. Vegetables that flourish in chilly temperatures include:

- Allium family members such as garlic, onions, leeks chives, and green onions
- Cabbage Broccoli, kale cauliflower, and Brussel sprouts
- Carrots, beets, parsnips, potatoes, and radishes
- Salad greens such as spinach, lettuce, and arugula

You may enjoy salads and fresh vegetables beginning in late autumn and extending well into April by shielding these crops from frost and supplying artificial illumination. More sunshine and warmer temperatures will naturally render your greenhouse uninhabitable to these cold-weather vegetables by the time spring comes.

It is time to swap them out with summer plants like zucchini, tomatoes, bell peppers, cucumbers, and beans. Vegetables that need a lot of areas, such as winter squash, maize, and melons, may not perform well in greenhouses.

Making a Tropical Greenhouse

Suppose your goal for a greenhouse is to have a genuine tropical greenhouse or "hothouse" that keeps warm regardless of the outside temperature. In that case, you will have to do a bit more preparation and be ready to pay the monthly electricity expenses that will undoubtedly accumulate. However, the result will be well worth it after you harvest tasty cucumbers, tomatoes, and fruits during the off-season.

The features of your greenhouse may vary depending on your demands and finances, but glass is a common building material for tropical greenhouses due to its ability to allow in a lot of light while still looking nice. According to the University of Georgia, Greenhouses should also feature fans or openings that can be conveniently opened for air as required. It will need specialized heaters and a cool humidifier in the winter to maintain acceptable humidity levels, but a cooling system or fans may be required in the summer. Your tropical greenhouse must also be well-insulated to guarantee that you're cooling, and heating efforts are not in vain.
You will also need a lot of grow lights in your tropical greenhouse. The farther north you are from the equator, the less sunshine you will get in winter. Exotic and summer plants want as much sunlight as possible, so grow lights will assist to make up the deficit and keep them growing throughout the year's shortest days.

Chapter 13 Tips on Pest & Disease Prevention

Even when plants are being prepped for transport, diseases and pests problems may cause havoc on greenhouse productivity. Taking the time to adequately manage diseases and pests may not be the major emphasis in the greenhouse during the spring when the to-do list appears never-ending. On the other hand, pests and diseases do not take a break, and dealing with them is critical to having a good spring.

Here are some ideas for dealing with pests and diseases during the busiest time of year:

1. Make sanitation a priority.

Sanitation is the primary line of protection against illness in any greenhouse. The disease is considerably more likely to spread in a greenhouse that is not clean and properly managed. Three methods for adequately sanitizing a greenhouse include weeding both in and out of the greenhouse, eliminating plant debris, and minimizing algae. It is also crucial to work on it methodically, day by day, rather than attempting to do it all at once. Making an action plan that includes particular things for certain staff might also be beneficial.

2. Recognize when your plants are at their most susceptible.

When there is water on the leaves, plants are more vulnerable to bacterial infections. The disease pressure may be less intense after the propagating stage than it was at the start of the process. However, plants might still be susceptible right before they are transported to retailers. Additionally, utilize the internet as a source to learn about various disorders. A quick search for whatever color spot you notice might give valuable track sheets, information cards, and advice for many disorders, albeit the diagnosis should be confirmed with a specialist. Place the data in a location where all workers may quickly access it. Also, take photographs of any plants you suspect are affected.

3. Complete your research.

In order to make the best selections, do research on bugs, pesticides, and other pest-related issues. Most greenhouse pest control methods include the use of insecticides. To choose the correct pesticide, you must first understand your intended goal, frequent greenhouse concerns, and schedule for getting plants ready to go

4. Determine which biocontrol agents will be most beneficial to your business.

Biological controls are intended to aid farmers. It might be tough to choose one since each one affects various pests in various ways.

5. Establish a consistent atmosphere.

Creating a constant atmosphere may not only help keep expenses down, but it could also help keep pests and illnesses at bay in your greenhouse. To maintain perfect growth conditions, wash fans, seal in heat, plus keep a check on temperature by adding updated thermometers and electronic controls. This procedure may take some time, so prepare ahead of time and distribute maintenance tasks to personnel as needed. Consider creating a checklist to ensure that no duty is overlooked and that your staff understands what is expected of them. In order to make the best selections, do research on pesticides, bugs, and other pest-related issues.

6. Gain knowledge from other farmers that are struggling with similar difficulties.

George's greenhouse finished its previous growing season in Ohio using just biological pest management. And they did not have a single illness problem when raising Christmas plants. George used a three-part pest and disease management routine that began during cutting and finished while growing in a 50,000 square foot facility. Ron Dorman, an assistant grower, came up with the concept for the program after attending a class at Five Star Greenhouses in Michigan. Take advantage of George's efforts by attending relevant seminars in your region. Call other farmers you met at Cultivate or other trade exhibitions to learn how to battle pests and diseases. Consider contacting extension workers at neighboring colleges since they have spent years researching the difficulties you are now dealing with.

7. Make scouting a priority.

Pest monitoring is a laborious, time-consuming activity that no farmer can do in a single day. Keeping rigorous and systematic scouting operations going even during the hectic spring season is critical. Check each plant row by row to ensure it is healthy. Examine the undersides of leaves for any insects or mites that may be lurking there. And start as soon as possible to give yourself more time to identify any harmful critters.

Chapter 14. Steps for starting a Greenhouse Business

You have identified the ideal company concept and are ready to go forward. Starting a company is more than merely registering with the state. Here is a straightforward approach to beginning a greenhouse company. It is important to prepare ahead, register correctly, and comply with the law.

14.1. Outline your greenhouse business

a: Make a plan

Successful entrepreneurship requires a clear strategy. It will assist you in laying out your company specifics and uncovering unknowns. Some key points to consider are:

- How much does it cost to startup?
- Who is your intended audience?
- How much can you charge?
- What will you name it?

Luckily, we did a lot of the legwork for you.

b. How much does it cost to start a greenhouse business?

Expenditures include the cost of building or renting the greenhouse, as well as labor and merchandise compensation.

c. How much does it cost to run a greenhouse?

You may construct your own greenhouse or rent one. A facility like this will probably be expensive. A large greenhouse requires a lot of land, which might cost several hundred thousand dollars. Renting such a place would likely cost multiple thousand dollars a month due to the need for so much room to produce and showcase your product. You will need to buy plants, food, seeds, flowers, and other landscaping and planting supplies. Charges for initial inventory are likely to be $4,000-$11,000, with monthly costs of $600-$1,500 or more. The precise number depends on greenhouse size.

electricity and Water are going to be several hundred dollars each month. Marketing expenditures should be budgeted at least $200 each month. Employees will need a minimum payment of $12 per hour, even more in certain locations. If you recruit marketing and accounting pros, expect to pay them $38,000-$55,000 annually.

d. Who is the intended audience?

The ideal client is a company owner in need of a varied selection of plants and flowers. Farmers, nursery operators, grocers, and florists are all examples. Additionally, greenhouse proprietors like to offer households with green thumbs. The objective is to sell a diverse selection of goods to each client to provide a steady supply of blooms, plants, food, and other veggies and keep inventory as fresh as possible.

e. Is there a limit on your charges?

Plant quality, attractiveness, lifespan, and other variables influence greenhouse product costs. Plants, flowers, and food may sell for a few dollars to over $110. Seeds range from 65 cents to a few bucks each package. Gardening and gardening products range from $7 to $60.

f. How profitable is a greenhouse business?

Greenhouses may be profitable in their first years, particularly if placed in a location where gardening, greenery, and wildlife are popular. A greenhouse might make $55,000-$110,000 per year. Profits may reach several hundred thousand dollars each year if the greenhouse owner grows and opens more sites.

g. How can you increase your profits?

In a greenhouse, a gardener or landscaper may offer tools including sprinklers, hand trowels, hoes, gardening gloves, pitchforks, shovels, tillers, loppers, cultivators, and soil. Selling floral and vegetable seeds may increase profits. Some greenhouse owners charge for delivery.

14.2. Create a legal entity

Sole proprietorship, LLC, partnership, and corporation are the most popular business structures. Creating a formal company organization like an LLC or corporation protects you from being sued personally.
Form Your LLC with a Professional Service
A nominal price may be paid to create an LLC yourself or to use one of the Best LLC Services. Your LLC will require a registered agent. Registered agent services are generally included in LLC formation packages. You may either employ or be your own registered agent.

14.3. File your Greenhouse Tax Return

Before starting a company, you must register for several federal and state taxes.
To register for taxes, you will need an EIN. It is simple and free! Your EIN may be obtained for free through the IRS fax, website, or mail. Depending on your company structure, you may have several tax alternatives. Example: Some LLCs may benefit from taxation as S corporations (S Corp). Your firm may be subject to unique state taxes.

14.4. Get a business bank deposit account & credit card

Open a business deposit account and get a credit card. Personal asset protection requires specialized business banking and credit accounts. If your business is sued, your personal assets (vehicle, house, and other possessions) are at stake. This is known as penetrating the corporate veil. Learning how to create company credit may also help you acquire better interest rates, larger credit lines, and more. This protects your personal belongings by distinguishing them from the company's assets. It simplifies bookkeeping and tax reporting.

14.5. Establish bookkeeping for your company

Understanding your business's financial success requires tracking your costs and profits. Detailed accounting also facilitates yearly tax filing. Obtain required permissions and licenses Failure to get required permissions and licenses may result in heavy penalties or even company closure. A greenhouse company may need state permissions and licensing. Visit SBA's licenses and permits reference to learn more about your state's regulations. Most companies must collect sales tax on their products or services.

Local licenses and permits:

- Contact your city, town, or county clerk.
- Contact one of the local business organizations mentioned in the US Small Business Associations database.

Occupancy Permit

A greenhouse, for example, requires a Certificate of Occupancy (CO). All construction rules, zoning laws, and government restrictions are satisfied by a CO. in renting a greenhouse; the landlord usually obtains a CO. Before leasing, verify that your landlord has or can get a valid CO for a greenhouse operation. A new CO is typically required after a large refurbishment. If your company is refurbished before opening, stipulate in your leasing agreement that payments will not begin until a valid CO is obtained.

Buying or building a greenhouse

You must get a valid CO from a local government body. Review all construction regulations and zoning criteria for your company site to guarantee compliance and CO eligibility.

14.6. Get Business Insurance

Your company requires insurance to operate safely and legally, like permits and licenses. Small business insurance protects your company's finances against insured losses.

There are many insurance plans designed for various company risks. If you are not clear about your company's risks, start with General Liability Insurance. This is the most common coverage needed by small companies and is a fantastic place to start. Workers' Compensation Insurance is another important product for many firms. If your company has workers, your state may require you to purchase Workers' Compensation insurance. Study how much business insurance for a greenhouse will cost.

14.7. Create Your Brand

Your brand is what your firm represents and how the public perceives it. A strong brand will help your company stand out. If you are not sure how to create a logo for your small company, check out free logo makers online.

How to advertise a greenhouse

Advertise your greenhouse company via local periodicals, billboards, radio, and TV advertisements. A user-friendly website showcasing your large selection will also assist. Invest in SEO to boost traffic to your website, social media channels, and blogs.

Establish your greenhouse as a credible brand deserving of client loyalty and confidence. If you please your first clients, they will tell their family and friends about your greenhouse. This is the finest type of free marketing.

How to retain customers

The greatest method to acquire and keep clients is to have a solid community reputation. A great selection, affordable pricing, and a pleasant crew will attract residents. Your flowers and plants must endure. If they die within days after purchase, buyers will spread the word that your items are of poor quality and not worth buying.

14.8: Make a business site

Create a website for your company after establishing your brand and designing your logo. Creating a website is important, but some people think they cannot achieve it because they lack web design skills. While this was a valid concern in 2014, online technology has advanced significantly in recent years, making the lives of small company owners much easier.

This is why you should not postpone constructing your website:

- Every genuine company has a website. Getting your company online does not matter what size or sector you are in.
- Tools like the GoDaddy Website Builder make constructing a basic website a breeze. You need not need a web developer or designer to build a great website.
- LinkedIn business profiles or Facebook pages are not a substitute for a company website.

14.9. Set up your company phone system.

Getting a business phone is one of the finest methods to keep your professional and personal lives separate. It also helps you automate your company, provides it respectability, and makes it simpler for prospective clients to identify and contact you. Many services are available to help entrepreneurs set up a company phone system. We compared the top firms on pricing, features, and user-friendliness.

Chapter 15 FAQs

15.1. How can a greenhouse's climate be controlled?

Humidity management enables the avoidance of dangerously lower or higher air humidity levels. When it comes to energy conservation, preventing excessive humidity is more critical. Humidity management may be accomplished by heating and/or ventilation. CO2 concentrations may be regulated by opening the greenhouse's top window.

15.2. What are the best conditions for growing plants inside a greenhouse?

Because the optimal temperature within the greenhouse is between 80- and 85-degrees Fahrenheit, perhaps the most critical lesson is to understand how to maintain a constant internal temperature.

15.3. What kinds of circumstances must greenhouses withstand?

Greenhouses Conserve Energy and Light. Plants need sunshine, warm temperatures, air, water, and nutrients to live and flourish. Each of these needs varies according to the plant.

15.4. Which variables must be regulated in a greenhouse to optimize plant growth?

Inside a greenhouse, the atmospheric variables that must be managed are the air temperature, relative humidity, and carbon dioxide (CO2) concentration. The latitude and duration of the greenhouse's operation will decide whether heating or cooling is the key priority or whether a mix of the two is necessary.

15.5. Which five environmental variables should be optimally regulated in a greenhouse?

The five determinants of environmental management in greenhouses

- Sunlight
- Temperature. Temperature is a critical component in plant

development.

- Humidity. Humidity is another critical component in sustaining plant development.
- The moisture content of the soil.
- CO_2

15.6. How is a greenhouse pest and disease controlled?

There are normally two techniques to manage pests and illnesses in a greenhouse. Every day throughout the growing season, the crop is carefully monitored, and if there is a feeling of pest or disease, the affected crop and surrounding crop are sprayed or drenched.

15.7. Is it necessary to shut the greenhouse entrance at night?

On bright days, open all doors and vents to maximize airflow. If the temperature continues high at night, they may be left open. Larger greenhouses may be equipped with automatic ventilation and shade for an additional expense.

15.8. What information do you need regarding greenhouses?

A greenhouse is a building that modifies the climate. It may be any size or form and has transparent walls and a roof, which allows the inside temperature to stay warmer than the outside temperature. Greenhouses are often constructed of glass, plastic, steel, and wood.

15.9. How does a greenhouse's temperature control system work?

The greenhouse sensory system is comprised of components that display and manage temperature, electrical conductivity, humidity, pH, carbon dioxide (c02), shading, and fogging, as well as reading external weather situations through a weather station

Conclusion

A greenhouse is a useful building for growing plants in a controlled environment. This atmosphere promotes rapid and healthy plant development regardless of the season.

Given the frequency with which you visit your greenhouse, especially during the summer, ensure that it is easily approachable and as close to the home as possible. Whether you are watering regularly, dampening down, opening, and closing vents and doors, or just stopping in to pick a few vegetables for your lunch, you will want it close at hand. Summer requires enough ventilation. A 6ft by 8ft greenhouse should ideally have two movable roof vents in addition to a side vent. It is worthwhile to invest in an automatic vent opener or to install your own.

Dampening down entails merely putting water over the greenhouse's bottom. Do this first thing in the morning - the water will evaporate during the day, creating humidity.

A solid, leveled floor, such as gravel on top of paving slabs of hardcore and sand, facilitates drainage and access and may be wetted (damped down) in the summer to keep the air humid. A soil border is an excellent method of growing greenhouse vegetables.

You can select the ideal greenhouses for different areas by following the suggestions provided below.

1. Land Area

How much space do you have available for a greenhouse? If you just have a little plot of land, you may experiment with smaller greenhouses or buildings with a lean-to style. Greater regions lend itself to larger constructions such as Gothic Arch or Ridge and Furrow.

2. Intensity of sunlight

Certain greenhouses are suited to locations with little sunshine, while others need high solar heat to promote plant development. The location determines the finest greenhouses for this case. For instance, if you live in a rocky area, you might choose an unequal span greenhouse.

3. Stability of the Ground

Not every surface is stable. Those with less stability need more robust frameworks made of metal or thick wood. In more stable places, plastic greenhouses may be built without concern. Additionally, you must find a site that allows water to drain quickly.

4. Climate Conditions

While a greenhouse may be put up anywhere, it is necessary to consider the meteorological conditions. Areas subject to months of snow are ideal for wood greenhouses, which aid in the retention of heat for the plants. On the other hand, windy places need heavy-duty metal frameworks to secure greenhouses to the ground.

One of the numerous benefits of a greenhouse is that it uses both supplementary lighting and natural sunshine (when available). Most high-value products, from decorative flowers to tomatoes, are

commercially grown in greenhouses for this same reason. Greenhouse cultivation, like indoor production, allows for numerous crops cycles each year.
However, like with any regulated environment, potential issue areas exist in greenhouses and must be monitored and handled proactively. Loss of control over your environment may result in cultivation difficulties ranging from inadequate airflow to excessive temperatures, as well as disease chances, such as watery viruses like Pythium.

You may also utilize your greenhouse to germinate seedlings before planting them outdoors. While you wait for the final frost to pass, your seedlings may be comfy and warm within the greenhouse, ready to transfer outside as soon as the weather permits. Once the seedlings have been transferred, direct sow another set of seeds in your garden for a staggered harvest.

However, not all fruit and veg like being transplanted. Some plants have delicate roots or struggle to adjust to the 0000temperature, humidity, and wind fluctuations that occur between the greenhouse and the garden. During this time, these delicate seedlings recover and start to grow robust. Their direct-sown seeds may have followed up to them, rendering the transplant effort pointless. The University of California, for example, suggests direct-sowing most root vegetables (000carrots, parsnips, beets, and so on), as well as cucumbers, melons, maize, peas (Pisum sativum), and beans.

Therefore, by adopting a "hardening off" procedure, utilizing biodegradable seed starting containers that allow the roots to stay undisturbed, and giving the seedlings a little additional pampering, if necessary, you may generate healthy seedlings. Peppers, Tomatoes, leafy greens, and cabbages are all wonderful choices for novices since they transfer readily.

Thank You

for purchasing my book! This book is
the result of years of experience and
dedication in my home garden.
I am very proud of it and
hope you enjoyed It!
If so, help me to spread the contents
by leaving a review that will give It
more insight. It will be of great help!!

Printed in Great Britain
by Amazon

16947531R00063